THE UPDATED U.S. CITIZENSHIP TEST WORKBOOK AND STUDY GUIDE

100 Practice USCIS Questions 2021 to 2024

Jeffrey B. Harris M.Ed

•YONAH PUBLISHING•

THE UPDATED U.S. CITIZENSHIP TEST
WORKBOOK and STUDY GUIDE: 100 USCIS
PRACTICE QUESTIONS 2021 TO 2024
BY JEFFREY B. HARRIS

Introduction

In order to become a citizen of the United States, there are four tests that you must pass:

1. Speaking Test

2. Reading test

3. Writing test

4. Civics test

Guess which one this book pertains to? Yes, civics. There are <u>100</u> potential questions that will be asked on the civics portion of the naturalization test. Usually, only <u>10</u> questions are asked, and you must answer <u>6</u> correctly. This book is set up to act as a study guide. The first half contains the questions and the second half contains the answers. You should write down the answer in the space provided once you truly know it. Good luck!

Information from www.uscis.gov

Reading Vocabulary Test

PEOPLE	Abraham Lincoln, George Washington
CIVICS	American Flag, Bill of Rights, Capital, Citizen, City, Congress, Country, Father of Our Country, Government, President, right, Senators, States, White House
PLACES	America, United States, U.S.
HOLIDAYS	Presidents' Day, Flag Day, Memorial Day, Independence Day, Labor Day, Thanksgiving, Columbus Day
QUESTION WORDS	How, What, When, Where, Who, Why
VERBS	Can, Come, Do/Does, Elects, Have/has, is/are/was/be, lives/lived, meet, name, pay, vote, want
OTHER (Function)	A, for, here, in, of, on, the, to, we
OTHER (Content)	Colors, Dollar Bill, First, Largest, Many, Most, North, One, People, Second, South

Writing Test

PEOPLE	ADAMS, LINCOLN, WASHINGTON
CIVICS	AMERICAN INDIANS, CAPITAL, CITIZENS, CIVIL WAR, CONGRESS, FATHER OF OUR COUNTRY, FLAG, FREE, FREEDOM OF SPEECH, PRESIDENT, RIGHT, SENATORS, STATE(S), WHITE HOUSE
PLACES	ALASKA, CALIFORNIA, CANADA, DELAWARE, MEXICO, NEW YORK CITY, UNITED STATES, WASHINGTON, WASHINGTON D.C.
MONTHS	JANUARY, FEBRUARY, MARCH, APRIL, MAY, JUNE, JULY, AUGUST, SEPTEMBER, OCTOBER, NOVEMBER, DECEMBER
HOLIDAYS	PRESIDENTS' DAY, FLAG DAY, MEMORIAL DAY, INDEPENDENCE DAY, LABOR DAY, THANKSGIVING, COLUMBUS DAY
VERBS	CAN, COME, DO/DOES, ELECTS, HAVE/HAS, IS/ARE/WAS/BE, LIVES/LIVED, MEET, NAME, PAY, VOTE, WANT
OTHER (FUNCTIONS)	AND, DURING, FOR, HERE, IN, OF, ON, THE, TO, WE
OTHER (CONTENT)	BLUE, DOLLAR BILL, FIFTY, FIRST, LARGEST, MOST, NORTH, ONE HUNDRED, PEOPLE, RED, SECOND, SOUTH, TAXES, WHITE

Naturalization Eligibility Requirements

Before an individual applies for naturalization, he or she must meet a few requirements. Depending on the individual's situation, there are different requirements that may apply. General requirements for naturalization are below.

Be at least 18 years old at the time of filing Form N-400, Application for Naturalization.

Be a permanent resident (have a "Green Card") for at least 5 years.

Show that you have lived for at least 3 months in the state or USCIS district where you apply.

Demonstrate continuous residence in the United States for at least 5 years immediately preceding the date of filing Form N-400.

Show that you have been physically present in the United States for at least 30 months out of the 5 years immediately preceding the date of filing Form N-400.

Be able to read, write, and speak basic English.

Have a basic understanding of U.S. history and government (civics).

Be a person of good moral character.

Demonstrate an attachment to the principles and ideals of the U.S. Constitution.

CIVICS QUESTIONS

1

WHAT IS CONSIDERED THE SUPREME LAW OF THE LAND?

2

WHAT IS THE FUNCTION OF THE CONSTITUTION?

3

WHAT ARE THE FIRST THREE WORDS OF THE CONSTITUTION, THAT REPRESENT THE IDEA OF SELF-GOVERNMENT?

4

WHAT'S AN AMENDMENT?

5

WHAT ARE THE FIRST TEN AMENDMENTS TO THE CONSTITUTION CALLED?

6

WHAT IS ONE FREEDOM FROM THE FIRST AMENDMENT?

7

HOW MANY AMENDMENTS ARE IN THE CONSTITUTION?

8

What did the Declaration of Independence do?

9

What are three rights in the Declaration of Independence?

10

What is freedom of religion?

11

What is the economic system in the United States?

12

What is the "rule of law"?

13

Name a branch of the U.S. government.

14

What stops a branch of government from becoming too powerful?

15
Who runs the executive branch?

16
Who makes federal laws?

17
What are the two parts of the U.S. Congress?

18
How many U.S. Senators are there?

19
A U.S. Senator is elected for how many years?

20
Who is one of your state's U.S. Senators now?

21
How many voting members are in the House of Representatives?

22

A U.S. REPRESENTATIVE IS ELECTED FOR HOW MANY YEARS?

23

NAME A U.S. REPRESENTATIVE FROM YOUR STATE.

24

WHO DOES A U.S. SENATOR REPRESENT?

25

WHY DO SOME STATES HAVE MORE REPRESENTATIVES THAN OTHER STATES?

26

A PRESIDENT IS ELECTED FOR HOW MANY YEARS?

27

WHAT MONTH DO WE VOTE FOR PRESIDENT?

28

WHO IS THE PRESIDENT OF THE UNITED STATES NOW?

29

Who is the Vice President of the United States now?

30

If the President can no longer serve, who becomes President?

31

Who will become president If both the President and the Vice President can no longer serve?

32

Who is the Commander in Chief of the military?

33

Who signs bills to become laws?

34

Who vetoes bills?

35

What does the President's Cabinet do?

36

What are two Cabinet-level positions?

37

What does the judicial branch do?

38

What is the highest court in the United States?

39

How many justices are on the Supreme Court?

40

Who is the Chief Justice of the United States now?

41

Under our Constitution, some powers belong to the federal government. What is one power of the federal government?

42

Under our Constitution, some powers belong to the states. What is one power of the states?

43

WHO IS THE GOVERNOR OF YOUR STATE NOW?

44

WHAT IS THE CAPITAL OF YOUR STATE?

45

WHAT ARE THE TWO MAJOR POLITICAL PARTIES IN THE UNITED STATES?

46

WHAT IS THE POLITICAL PARTY OF THE PRESIDENT NOW?

47

WHAT IS THE NAME OF THE SPEAKER OF THE HOUSE OF REPRESENTATIVES NOW?

48

THERE ARE FOUR AMENDMENTS TO THE CONSTITUTION ABOUT WHO CAN VOTE. DESCRIBE ONE OF THEM.

49

WHAT IS ONE RESPONSIBILITY THAT IS ONLY FOR
UNITED STATES CITIZENS?

50

NAME ONE RIGHT ONLY FOR UNITED STATES CITIZENS.

51

WHAT ARE TWO RIGHTS OF EVERYONE LIVING IN THE
UNITED STATES?

52

WHAT DO WE SHOW LOYALTY TO WHEN WE SAY THE
PLEDGE OF ALLEGIANCE?

53

WHAT IS <u>ONE</u> PROMISE YOU MAKE WHEN YOU BECOME A
UNITED STATES CITIZEN?

54

HOW OLD DO CITIZENS HAVE TO BE TO VOTE FOR
PRESIDENT?

55
WHAT ARE TWO WAYS THAT AMERICANS CAN PARTICIPATE IN THEIR DEMOCRACY?

56
WHEN IS THE LAST DAY YOU CAN SEND IN FEDERAL INCOME TAX FORMS?

57
WHEN MUST ALL MEN REGISTER FOR THE SELECTIVE SERVICE?

58
WHAT IS ONE REASON COLONISTS CAME TO AMERICA?

59
WHO LIVED IN AMERICA BEFORE THE EUROPEANS ARRIVED?

60
WHAT GROUP OF PEOPLE WAS TAKEN TO AMERICA AND SOLD AS SLAVES?

61
WHY DID THE COLONISTS FIGHT THE BRITISH?

62

WHO WROTE THE DECLARATION OF INDEPENDENCE?

63

WHEN WAS THE DECLARATION OF INDEPENDENCE ADOPTED?

64

THERE WERE 13 ORIGINAL STATES. NAME THREE.

65

WHAT HAPPENED AT THE CONSTITUTIONAL CONVENTION?

66

WHEN WAS THE CONSTITUTION WRITTEN?

67

THE FEDERALIST PAPERS SUPPORTED THE PASSAGE OF THE U.S. CONSTITUTION. NAME THE WRITERS.

68

WHAT IS SOMETHING BENJAMIN FRANKLIN IS FAMOUS FOR?

69

WHO IS THE "FATHER OF OUR COUNTRY"?

70

WHO WAS THE FIRST PRESIDENT?

71

WHAT TERRITORY DID THE UNITED STATES BUY FROM FRANCE IN 1803?

72

NAME A WAR FOUGHT BY THE UNITED STATES IN THE 1800s.

73

NAME THE U.S. WAR BETWEEN THE NORTH AND THE SOUTH.

74

NAME A PROBLEM THAT LED TO THE CIVIL WAR.

75

WHAT WAS AN IMPORTANT THING THAT ABRAHAM LINCOLN DID?

76

What did the Emancipation Proclamation do?

77

What did Susan B. Anthony do?

78

Name a war fought by the United States in the 1900s.

79

Who was President during World War I?

80

Who was President during the Great Depression and World War II?

81

Who did the United States fight in World War II?

82

Before he was President, Eisenhower was a general. What war was he in?

83

During the Cold War, what was the main concern of the United States?

84

What movement tried to end racial discrimination?

85

What did Martin Luther King, Jr. do?

86

What major event happened on September 11, 2001, in the United States?

87

Name one American Indian tribe in the United States.

88

Name the two longest rivers in the United States.

89

WHAT OCEAN IS ON THE WEST COAST OF THE UNITED STATES?

90

WHAT OCEAN IS ON THE EAST COAST OF THE UNITED STATES?

91

NAME A U.S. TERRITORY.

92

NAME A STATE THAT BORDERS CANADA.

93

NAME A STATE THAT BORDERS MEXICO.

94

WHAT IS THE CAPITAL OF THE UNITED STATES?

95

WHERE IS THE STATUE OF LIBERTY?

96
WHY DOES THE FLAG HAVE 13 STRIPES?

97
WHY DOES THE FLAG HAVE 50 STARS?

98
WHAT IS THE NAME OF THE NATIONAL ANTHEM?

99
WHEN DO WE CELEBRATE INDEPENDENCE DAY?

100
NAME TWO NATIONAL U.S. HOLIDAYS.

ANSWERS

1
THE CONSTITUTION

2
SETS UP THE GOVERNMENT
DEFINES THE GOVERNMENT
PROTECTS BASIC RIGHTS OF AMERICANS

3
WE THE PEOPLE

4
A CHANGE OR ADDITION TO THE CONSTITUTION

5
THE BILL OF RIGHTS

6
SPEECH
RELIGION
ASSEMBLY
PRESS
PETITION THE GOVERNMENT

7
TWENTY-SEVEN

8
SAID THAT THE UNITED STATES IS FREE FROM GREAT BRITAIN

9
LIFE
LIBERTY
PURSUIT OF HAPPINESS

10
YOU CAN PRACTICE (OR NOT PRACTICE) ANY RELIGION.

11
CAPITALIST OR MARKET ECONOMY

12
EVERYONE (INCLUDING THE GOVERNMENT) MUST FOLLOW THE LAW.

13
LEGISLATIVE
EXECUTIVE
JUDICIAL

14
CHECKS AND BALANCES
SEPARATION OF POWERS

15
THE PRESIDENT

16
CONGRESS
SENATE AND HOUSE OF REPRESENTATIVES
U.S. LEGISLATURE

17
SENATE AND HOUSE OF REPRESENTATIVES

18
ONE HUNDRED

19
SIX

20

ANSWERS WILL VARY.

21

FOUR HUNDRED THIRTY-FIVE

22

TWO

23

ANSWERS WILL VARY. SEE APPENDIX.

24

ALL PEOPLE OF THE STATE

25

BECAUSE OF THE STATE'S POPULATION

26

FOUR

27

NOVEMBER

28

JOE BIDEN

29

KAMALA HARRIS

30

THE VICE PRESIDENT

31

THE SPEAKER OF THE HOUSE

32
THE PRESIDENT

33
THE PRESIDENT

34
THE PRESIDENT

35
ADVISES THE PRESIDENT

36
SECRETARY OF AGRICULTURE
SECRETARY OF COMMERCE
SECRETARY OF DEFENSE
SECRETARY OF EDUCATION
SECRETARY OF ENERGY
SECRETARY OF HEALTH AND HUMAN SERVICES
SECRETARY OF HOMELAND SECURITY
SECRETARY OF HOUSING AND URBAN DEVELOPMENT
SECRETARY OF THE INTERIOR
SECRETARY OF LABOR
SECRETARY OF STATE
SECRETARY OF TRANSPORTATION
SECRETARY OF THE TREASURY
SECRETARY OF VETERANS AFFAIRS
ATTORNEY GENERAL
VICE PRESIDENT

37
REVIEWS LAWS
EXPLAINS LAWS
RESOLVES DISAGREEMENTS
DECIDES IF A LAW GOES AGAINST THE CONSTITUTION

38
THE SUPREME COURT

39

NINE

40

JOHN ROBERTS (JOHN G. ROBERTS, JR.)

41

TO PRINT MONEY
TO DECLARE WAR
TO CREATE AN ARMY
TO MAKE TREATIES

42

PROVIDE SCHOOLING AND EDUCATION
PROVIDE PROTECTION (POLICE)
PROVIDE SAFETY (FIRE DEPARTMENTS)
GIVE A DRIVER'S LICENSE
APPROVE ZONING AND LAND USE

43

ANSWERS WILL VARY.

44

ANSWERS WILL VARY.

45

DEMOCRATIC AND REPUBLICAN

46

REPUBLICAN

47

2021- NANCY PELOSI (SUBJECT TO CHANGE)

48

CITIZENS EIGHTEEN (18) AND OLDER CAN VOTE.
YOU DON'T HAVE TO PAY A POLL TAX TO VOTE.
ANY CITIZEN CAN VOTE.
A MALE CITIZEN OF ANY RACE CAN VOTE.

49

SERVE ON A JURY
VOTE IN A FEDERAL ELECTION

50

VOTE IN A FEDERAL ELECTION
RUN FOR FEDERAL OFFICE

51

FREEDOM OF EXPRESSION
FREEDOM OF SPEECH
FREEDOM OF ASSEMBLY
FREEDOM TO PETITION THE GOVERNMENT
FREEDOM OF RELIGION
THE RIGHT TO BEAR ARMS

52

THE UNITED STATES
THE FLAG

53

GIVE UP LOYALTY TO OTHER COUNTRIES
DEFEND THE CONSTITUTION AND LAWS OF THE U.S
OBEY THE LAWS OF THE UNITED STATES
SERVE IN THE U.S. MILITARY
SERVE THE NATION
BE LOYAL TO THE UNITED STATES

54

EIGHTEEN (18) AND OLDER

55

VOTE
JOIN A POLITICAL PARTY
HELP WITH A CAMPAIGN
JOIN A CIVIC GROUP
JOIN A COMMUNITY GROUP
GIVE AN ELECTED OFFICIAL YOUR OPINION ON AN ISSUE
CALL SENATORS AND REPRESENTATIVES

PUBLICLY SUPPORT OR OPPOSE AN ISSUE OR POLICY
RUN FOR OFFICE
WRITE TO A NEWSPAPER

56
APRIL 15

57
AT AGE EIGHTEEN
BETWEEN EIGHTEEN AND TWENTY-SIX

58
FREEDOM
POLITICAL LIBERTY
RELIGIOUS FREEDOM
ECONOMIC OPPORTUNITY
PRACTICE THEIR RELIGION
ESCAPE PERSECUTION

59
AMERICAN INDIANS
NATIVE AMERICANS

60
AFRICANS
PEOPLE FROM AFRICA

61
BECAUSE OF HIGH TAXES (TAXATION WITHOUT REPRESENTATION)
BECAUSE THE BRITISH ARMY STAYED IN THEIR HOUSES (BOARDING, QUARTERING)
BECAUSE THEY DIDN'T HAVE SELF-GOVERNMENT

62
(THOMAS) JEFFERSON

63
JULY 4, 1776

64
NEW HAMPSHIRE
MASSACHUSETTS
RHODE ISLAND
CONNECTICUT
NEW YORK
NEW JERSEY
PENNSYLVANIA
DELAWARE
MARYLAND
VIRGINIA
NORTH CAROLINA
SOUTH CAROLINA
GEORGIA

65
THE CONSTITUTION WAS WRITTEN.
THE FOUNDING FATHERS WROTE THE CONSTITUTION.

66
1787

67
JAMES MADISON
ALEXANDER HAMILTON
JOHN JAY
PUBLIUS

68
U.S. DIPLOMAT
OLDEST MEMBER OF THE CONSTITUTIONAL CONVENTION
FIRST POSTMASTER GENERAL OF THE UNITED STATES
WRITER OF "POOR RICHARD'S ALMANAC"
STARTED THE FIRST FREE LIBRARIES

69
GEORGE WASHINGTON

70
GEORGE WASHINGTON

71
THE LOUISIANA TERRITORY
LOUISIANA

72
WAR OF 1812
MEXICAN-AMERICAN WAR
CIVIL WAR
SPANISH-AMERICAN WAR

73
THE CIVIL WAR
THE WAR BETWEEN THE STATES

74
SLAVERY
ECONOMIC REASONS
STATES' RIGHTS

75
FREED THE SLAVES
PRESERVED THE UNION
LED THE UNITED STATES DURING THE CIVIL WAR

76
FREED SLAVES IN THE CONFEDERACY
FREED SLAVES IN THE CONFEDERATE STATES
FREED SLAVES IN MOST SOUTHERN STATES

77
FOUGHT FOR WOMEN'S RIGHTS
FOUGHT FOR CIVIL RIGHTS

78

WORLD WAR I
WORLD WAR II
KOREAN WAR
VIETNAM WAR
(PERSIAN) GULF WAR

79

WOODROW WILSON

80

FRANKLIN ROOSEVELT

81

JAPAN, GERMANY, AND ITALY

82

WORLD WAR II

83

COMMUNISM

84

CIVIL RIGHTS (MOVEMENT)

85

FOUGHT FOR CIVIL RIGHTS
WORKED FOR EQUALITY FOR ALL AMERICANS

86

TERRORISTS ATTACKED THE UNITED STATES.

87

CHEROKEE
NAVAJO
SIOUX
CHIPPEWA

CHOCTAW
PUEBLO
APACHE
IROQUOIS
CREEK
BLACKFEET
SEMINOLE
CHEYENNE
ARAWAK
SHAWNEE
MOHEGAN
HURON
ONEIDA
LAKOTA
CROW
TETON
HOPI
INUIT

88
MISSOURI (RIVER)
MISSISSIPPI (RIVER)

89
PACIFIC (OCEAN)

90
ATLANTIC (OCEAN)

91
PUERTO RICO
U.S. VIRGIN ISLANDS
AMERICAN SAMOA
NORTHERN MARIANA ISLANDS
GUAM

92
MAINE
NEW HAMPSHIRE
VERMONT

New York
Pennsylvania
Ohio
Michigan
Minnesota
North Dakota
Montana
Idaho
Washington
Alaska

93

California
Arizona
New Mexico
Texas

94

Washington, D.C.

95

New York (Harbor)
Liberty Island

96

because there were 13 original colonies
because the stripes represent the original colonies

97

because there is one star for each state
because each star represents a state
because there are 50 states

98

The Star-Spangled Banner

99

JULY 4

100

NEW YEAR'S DAY
MARTIN LUTHER KING, JR. DAY
PRESIDENTS' DAY
MEMORIAL DAY
INDEPENDENCE DAY
LABOR DAY
COLUMBUS DAY
VETERANS DAY
THANKSGIVING
CHRISTMAS

Appendix

20. List of U.S. Senators- subject to change

HTTP://WWW.SENATE.GOV/SENATORS/CONTACT/

23. List of U.S. Representatives- subject to change

HTTP://WWW.HOUSE.GOV/REPRESENTATIVES

43. List of State governors- subject to change

HTTP://WWW.NGA.ORG/CMS/GOVERNORS/BIOS

44. List of State Capitals

Alabama - Montgomery
Alaska - Juneau
Arizona - Phoenix
Arkansas - Little Rock
California - Sacramento
Colorado - Denver
Connecticut - Hartford
Delaware - Dover
Florida - Tallahassee
Georgia - Atlanta
Hawaii - Honolulu
Idaho - Boise
Illinois - Springfield
Indiana - Indianapolis
Iowa - Des Moines
Kansas - Topeka
Kentucky - Frankfort
Louisiana - Baton Rouge
Maine - Augusta
Maryland - Annapolis
Massachusetts - Boston
Michigan - Lansing

MINNESOTA - ST. PAUL
MISSISSIPPI - JACKSON
MISSOURI - JEFFERSON CITY
MONTANA - HELENA
NEBRASKA - LINCOLN
NEVADA - CARSON CITY
NEW HAMPSHIRE - CONCORD
NEW JERSEY - TRENTON
NEW MEXICO - SANTA FE
NEW YORK - ALBANY
NORTH CAROLINA - RALEIGH
NORTH DAKOTA - BISMARCK
OHIO - COLUMBUS
OKLAHOMA - OKLAHOMA CITY
OREGON - SALEM
PENNSYLVANIA - HARRISBURG
RHODE ISLAND - PROVIDENCE
SOUTH CAROLINA - COLUMBIA
SOUTH DAKOTA - PIERRE
TENNESSEE - NASHVILLE
TEXAS - AUSTIN
UTAH - SALT LAKE CITY
VERMONT - MONTPELIER
VIRGINIA - RICHMOND
WASHINGTON - OLYMPIA
WEST VIRGINIA - CHARLESTON
WISCONSIN - MADISON
WYOMING - CHEYENNE

More Practice

Multiple Choice

1. What is the form of government of the United States?
A. Direct Democracy   B. Autocracy
   C.   Parliamentary Republic   D. Federal Republic

2. What is the supreme law of the land?*
A. Declaration of Independence   B. Amendment
   C.   The Constitution   D. Articles of Confederation

3. The U.S. Constitution does not
A. Explain the functions of Government
B. Protect the citizens of the US
C. Define the powers of government
D. Include any amendments

4. The U.S. Constitution starts with the words "We the People." "We the People" does not mean
A. The consent of the governed
B. Only the people born in America
C. Popular sovereignty
D. People should govern themselves

5. How are changes made to the U.S. Constitution?
A. Popular vote   B. Amendments
   C.   26 States vote   D. 51 votes in the Senate

6. Which answer best explains whom the Bill of Rights protect?
A. Rights of Americans   B. Rights of the President
   C.   Rights of Senators   D. Rights of those in power

7. How many amendments does the U.S. Constitution have?*
A. 10   B. 23   C. 27   D. 19

8. What founding document said the American colonies were free from Britain?
A. Declaration of Independence   B. Magna Carta
   C.   Mayflower Compact   D. The Constitution

Short Answer

9. Why is the Declaration of Independence important?

_____

10. NAME TWO IMPORTANT IDEAS FROM THE DECLARATION OF INDEPENDENCE AND THE U.S. CONSTITUTION.

_____

_____

11. THE WORDS "LIFE, LIBERTY, AND THE PURSUIT OF HAPPINESS" ARE IN WHAT FOUNDING DOCUMENT?

_____

12. WHAT IS THE ECONOMIC SYSTEM OF THE UNITED STATES?*

_____

13. WHAT IS THE RULE OF LAW?

_____

TRUE OR FALSE

14. MANY DOCUMENTS INFLUENCED THE U.S. CONSTITUTION, INCLUDING THE THE IROQUOIS GREAT LAW OF PEACE.
_____
IF FALSE, WRITE THE CORRECT
ANSWER_____

15. THERE ARE THREE BRANCHES OF GOVERNMENT BECAUSE EVEN NUMBERS WOULD BE A TIE. _____
IF FALSE, WRITE THE CORRECT
ANSWER_____

16. ONE OF THE THREE BRANCHES OF GOVERNMENT IS THE CONSTITUTION. _____
IF FALSE, WRITE THE CORRECT
ANSWER_____

17. THE PRESIDENT OF THE UNITED STATES IS IN CHARGE OF THE EXECUTIVE BRANCH OF GOVERNMENT._____
IF FALSE, WRITE THE CORRECT
ANSWER_____

18. THE PART OF THE FEDERAL GOVERNMENT THAT WRITES LAWS IS THE JUDICIAL BRANCH. _____
IF FALSE, WRITE THE CORRECT
ANSWER_____

19. THE TWO PARTS OF THE U.S. CONGRESS ARE THE HOUSE OF COMMONS AND THE SENATE. _____

If false, write the correct
answer_____

20. One power of the Executive Branch is to enforce the law.
_____
If false, write the correct
answer_____

Fill in the blank

21. There are _____ U.S. senators.

22. A term for a U.S. senator lasts _____ years.

23. _____ is one of your state's U.S. senators now?

24. There are _____ voting members in the House of Representatives.

25. A term for a member of the House of Representatives is _____ years.

Short Answer

26. Why do U.S. representatives serve shorter terms than U.S. senators?

27. How many senators does each state have?

28. Why does each state have two senators?

29. Name your U.S. representative.

30. What is the name of the Speaker of the House of Representatives now?*

31. Who does a U.S. senator represent?

32. Who elects U.S. senators?

33. WHO DOES A MEMBER OF THE HOUSE OF REPRESENTATIVES REPRESENT?

TRUE OR FALSE

34. THE PRESIDENT ELECTS MEMBERS OF THE HOUSE OF REPRESENTATIVES._____
 IF FALSE, WRITE THE CORRECT
ANSWER_____

35. SOME STATES HAVE MORE REPRESENTATIVES THAN OTHER STATES BECAUSE OF HIGHER POPULATIONS. _____
 IF FALSE, WRITE THE CORRECT
ANSWER_____

36. THE PRESIDENT OF THE UNITED STATES IS ELECTED FOR SIX YEARS_____
 IF FALSE, WRITE THE CORRECT
ANSWER_____

37. THE PRESIDENT OF THE UNITED STATES CAN SERVE ONLY TWO TERMS SO HE/SHE DOESN'T GET TOO POWERFUL. _____
 IF FALSE, WRITE THE CORRECT
ANSWER_____

38. MIKE PENCE IS THE NAME OF THE PRESIDENT OF THE UNITED STATES NOW. _____
 IF FALSE, WRITE THE CORRECT
ANSWER_____

39. KAMALA HARRIS IS THE NAME OF THE VICE PRESIDENT OF THE UNITED STATES NOW. _____
 IF FALSE, WRITE THE CORRECT
ANSWER_____

MULTIPLE CHOICE

40. IF THE PRESIDENT CAN NO LONGER SERVE, WHO BECOMES PRESIDENT?
A. VICE PRESIDENT   B. SECRETARY OF STATE
    C.   SPEAKER OF THE HOUSE   D. SECRETARY OF DEFENSE

41. WHICH IS NOT ONE POWER OF THE PRESIDENT.
A. SIGN LAWS B. ENFORCE LAWS
    C.   CHIEF DIPLOMAT   D. MAKE LAWS

42. WHO IS COMMANDER IN CHIEF OF THE U.S. MILITARY?

A. Secretary of Defense B. President
  c.   Vice President   D. Secretary of State

43. Who signs bills to become laws?
A. Senators B. Congressmen
  c. President   D. Vice President

44. Who vetoes bills?*
A. Senators B. Congressmen
  c. President   D. Vice President

45. Who appoints federal judges?
A. Senators B. Congressmen
  c. President   D. Vice President

46. The executive branch has many parts. Which is not one?
A. President B. Cabinet
  c. Senate   D. Federal Agencies

Short Answer

47. What does the President's Cabinet do?

48. What are two Cabinet-level positions?

49. Why is the Electoral College important?

50. What is one part of the judicial branch?

Answers

1. D. Federal Republic
 Or Constitution-based federal republic
Representative democracy

2. C. (U.S.) Constitution

3. D. Include any amendments
What it does: Forms the government
Defines powers of government
Defines the parts of government
Protects the rights of the people

4. B. Only people born in America
It means: Self-government
Popular sovereignty
Consent of the governed
People should govern themselves
(Example of) social contract

5. B. Amendments
Or the amendment process

6. A. (The basic) rights of Americans
(The basic) rights of people living in the United States

7. C. Twenty-seven (27)

8. A. Declaration of Independence

9. It says America is free from British control.
It says all people are created equal.
It identifies inherent rights.
It identifies individual freedoms.

10. Equality
Liberty
Social contract
Natural rights
Limited government
Self-government

11. Declaration of Independence

12. Capitalism
Free market economy

13. Everyone must follow the law.

Leaders must obey the law.
Government must obey the law.
No one is above the law.

14. True
Declaration of Independence
Articles of Confederation
Federalist Papers
Anti-Federalist Papers
Virginia Declaration of Rights
Fundamental Orders of Connecticut
Mayflower Compact
Iroquois Great Law of Peace

15. False
So one part does not become too powerful
Checks and balances
Separation of powers

16. False
Legislative, executive, and judicial
Congress, president, and the courts

17. True
Executive branch

18. False
(U.S.) Congress
(U.S. or national) legislature
Legislative branch

19. False
Senate and House (of Representatives)

20. True
Writes laws
Declares war
Makes the federal budget

21. One hundred (100)

22. Six (6) years

23. Answers will vary. [District of Columbia residents and residents of U.S. territories should answer that D.C. (or the territory where the applicant lives) has no U.S. senators.]

24. Four hundred thirty-five (435)

25. Two (2) years

26. To more closely follow public opinion

27. Two (2)

28. Equal representation (for small states)
The Great Compromise (Connecticut Compromise)

29. Answers will vary.

30. Visit uscis.gov/citizenship/testupdates for the name of the Speaker of the House of Representatives. 2021- Pelosi

31. Citizens of their state

32. Citizens from their state

33. Citizens in their (congressional) district
Citizens in their district

34. False- Citizens from their (congressional) district elect representatives

35. True (Because of) the state's population
(Because) they have more people
(Because) some states have more people

36. False- Four (4) years

37. True- or (Because of) the 22nd Amendment
To keep the president from becoming too powerful

38. False- Visit uscis.gov/citizenship/testupdates for the name of the President of the United States. Now-Joe Biden

39. True- Visit uscis.gov/citizenship/testupdates for the name of the Vice President of the United States.

40. A. The Vice President (of the United States)

41. D. Makes Laws, that's the Legislative Branch.
The President: Signs bills into law
Vetoes bills
Enforces laws
Is Commander in Chief (of the military)
Is Chief diplomat

42. B. The President (of the United States)

43. C. The President (of the United States)

44. C. The President (of the United States)

45. C. The President (of the United States)

46. C. Senate is incorrect. The executive branch includes:
President (of the United States)
Cabinet
Federal departments and agencies

47. Advises the President (of the United States)

48. Attorney General
Secretary of Agriculture
Secretary of Commerce
Secretary of Defense
Secretary of Education
Secretary of Energy
Secretary of Health and Human Services
Secretary of Homeland Security
Secretary of Housing and Urban Development
Secretary of the Interior
Secretary of Labor
Secretary of State
Secretary of Transportation
Secretary of the Treasury
Secretary of Veterans Affairs
Vice President (of the United States)

49. It decides who is elected president.
It provides a compromise between the popular election of the
president and congressional selection.

50. Supreme Court or Federal Courts

Made in the USA
Las Vegas, NV
05 April 2021